Blueberry Fool

Blueberry Fool

Memory, Moments, and Meaning

THOM ROCK

RESOURCE *Publications* · Eugene, Oregon

BLUEBERRY FOOL
Memory, Moments, and Meaning

Resource Publications
An Imprint of Wipf and Stock Publishers
199 W. 8th Ave., Suite 3
Eugene, OR 97401
www.wipfandstock.com

ISBN 13: 978-1-61097-448-6

Manufactured in the U.S.A.

Some of the essays in this collection were previously published:
  "How I Wonder What You Are" (in different form) was first
published in *Yankee Magazine*.
  "Hark" appeared originally in the anthology, *A Bird in the Hand:
Risk and Flight,* Outrider Press.
  An abridged version of "Preservation" was published in the
anthology, *Cupcakes on the Counter: The Stoves and Stories of our
Families*, as well as in its original form in *Yankee Magazine*.

The author wishes to thank the editors of these publications.

For Jim, always, who first saw the fool in me.
It takes one to know one.

So vast, so limitless in capacity is man's imagination to disperse and burn away the rubble-dross of fact and probability, leaving only truth and dream.

—WILLIAM FAULKNER

Contents

The Gospel according to Blueberry

QUICK THEN, in bog or fen, in barren, field or meadow, in the bottomlands or uplands or on the sides of mountains, before drought or ground-soaking rain, in warm or cool currents of air, before early or late frost, before snowfall, before the footfall of foragers, before the light-footed scurry of the white-footed mouse or the long towering night of the black bear approaches, before bright day-flying moths and their caterpillars spin, before the elfin, the swallowtail, the sphinx, before spore, before fungus, before gall, before rot or blight; drink in each dazzling day and star-strewn night, fill yourself with the wild wind, or the fireweed's flame, with the fragrance of summer cloud and spruce, or turn blue trying. Become soft, become sweet, become sky.

Now and Then

THE BERRIES ripen in such abundance; I bow and bend in their presence. Having quickly learned the harvesting work my fingers do so all on their own, leaving my mind to wander. And where it wanders to most often is memory. One moment I am aware of the summer sun on my back, my hands working away in the tangle of berry, leaf, and twig. The next: a flock of memories have ghosted their way into the meadow. Whether or not the repetitive motions and the sound of berries falling into bucket influence this phenomenon I do not know. But when I am out there in the meadow filling a tin pail with those indigo gems, time ceases to march in an orderly fashion, sometimes standing still, but more often than not sliding backwards in a moonwalk of memory. Moments from time appear unbidden and as mysterious as question marks interwoven amongst the grasses and goldenrods. I find myself in the past, or at least in the company of those who inhabit it. Do I somehow transport myself to them, I wonder, or is it they who come to me?

Our lives are made of moments in time. And, at the same time, everything is memory save for that slimmest slip of time that just now slipped by. Yet we order our lives around the façade of the calendar, the upswing of the pendulum, the accuracy and endurance of memory. We separate past and present as if they were opposing notions. We feebly attempt to mark and measure our days regardless of whether they stretch out lazily in the long summer sun or curl up tight under winter's equally long night. They pile up behind us: a handful of years, a thousand moons, until eventually time seems to fly and moments appear to pass by more quickly. You reach beneath a berry branch one morning and find not your own fingers stretching out for the blue from the cuff of your sleeve but those of your father's work-worn hands.

In those moments I am no longer in this northern meadow but seated at the old oak table at a family reunion; my mother setting the table with her mother's favorite china painted with tiny blue forget-me-nots, my sister and I arguing over which of us should get to sit on the high wooden stool, its rickety legs bound and reinforced with baling wire. Or I'm walking up the dirt road with my family one long-ago evening catching fireflies with my sister. Or I catch a glimpse through the sweet steam of my mother laughing with her brothers, maple sap boiling wildly before them in the broad, flat metal pan in the middle of the sugarhouse, in the middle of the woods.

There have indeed been times in this time-lost meadow when I have plucked a particularly sweet memory from these berry bushes and held it wonderingly in my palm, not ever wanting to let it go. But memory, like time, is always moving, even when we'd rather stand still. I know I cannot inhabit the past, or at least if I choose to do so exclusively I run the risk of missing out on those moments that might, in turn, become my future memories. Or in other words: my life. But holding on to a memory is not the same as inhabiting the past, and a vivid moment can return us to its illuminating source if only for a moment.

And yet those sweet moments seem to spring up suddenly and apart from no obvious pattern. With no clear warning a memory might swell, blossom, and bear fruit in the blueberry barren. The wind teasing the tall grasses just so, a certain breath of air, or the sound of travelling geese journeying high above . . . and suddenly I am inexplicably somewhere else, in a place and time that no longer is. Not exactly a then-and-there but a then-again. A long-lost summer afternoon, a rope swing swung over an arcing branch. An iconic image that appears frozen in time, like an unsuspecting fly stuck in amber. Yet these fragments of memory are fleeting: despite their crystalline cells, they still hum and whir. They can even take flight.

Which is it, then: is memory moving or static? Is it a fossilized jewel kept inside some velvet-lined treasure box to be taken out at will and admired? Or might it be something equally delicate but surely winged, an ever-evolving insect capable of metamorphosis and migration? Either way, I'd like to believe these moments will never fade away, but memory also has a trick up its sleeve: it can disappear in the wink of an eye. So I line the fluttering memories up across the page syllable after syllable to make of them something indelible. Something to believe in.

Even if memory is a time-traveler, a shapeshifter, it is what I believe in. What we remember and how we remember it shapes the story of our lives, of who we are. When we call forth moments from our individual journeys, or when they arrive unbidden, we cannot help attaching to them meaning and definition. The past becomes present in the present as well as the future: we become our memories.

I believe in memory because at the sight of a single firefly it carries me, in a flash, over and through time to a long-ago velvet night. I believe in memory because I have felt in the meadow, as real and present as if I were a child again, my own mother's hand pressed upon my chest. I believe in memory because I also believe that death is not the end of our story. That the story of everyone I have ever loved continues, their story and mine, beyond what we presume to be "the end." Admittedly, I am uneasy stating this belief; I am not entirely comfortable defining myself as a person of belief, of faith. What are the implications of saying, for example, that I believe love lives on, that we live on? Am I automatically embracing a belief that heaven exists and is where my beloveds abide? I'm not really sure. Nor can I state with unwavering trust that I believe in the power of prayer. Yet if I do not recognize the moments from time that appear to me in the meadow as just that—as grace-filled prayers—well, the alternative is disconcerting at the very least. If faith equals certainty, I am undoubtedly uneasy, for I cannot grasp how I might ever prove how meaningfully I have experienced memory amidst a hillside of wild blueberries.

Still, I cannot imagine myself saying, "I do *not* believe."

Borderlands

THE SUMMER fields are painted ochre and saffron. The goldenrod seem to know instinctively just when to stretch their willowy limbs and unfurl their blazing petals all on their own. Black-eyed Susans accompany the golden spires in some places, while in others oxeye daisies keep watch. The embers of fireweed glimmer here and there and the sweet globes of milkweed flowers are luring insects small and large to their fragrant world. The wild blueberries are coming in, ripening not from cultivation or savvy hybridization, but from something in the summer air: birdsong, perhaps. At least that's what I think as I squat in the lower field picking the tiny indigo bubbles from the low-growing plants.

I walk upright to this wild place. My nifty opposable thumbs make berry picking a snap. But other than my harvesting presence I am not a factor in this meadowland; I have neither planted nor tended these bushes. The berries I drop into the basket exist entirely due to the bees that pollinated the waxy white flowers earlier in the spring. I am an outsider here, a visitor in this miraculous, blue world. I neither speak the blueberry tongue nor know the lapis language of bee and flower. An entire insect world clicks and whirs invisibly in the grasses that weave in and out of this blue treasure trove. The morning chorus of birds slides elemental over the spruce trees. I imagine in the sweet gibberish of their song a joyful hymn offered at the resurrection of daylight, but who knows, maybe their melodious notes are merely orders, something as simple and mundane as today's to-do list?

The other night I awoke to eerie, wild words that left me feeling unsettled and disoriented. So foreign to me was their language that I could not even assure myself, "Only a fox barking, or the screech of owl." What creature should speak such syllables to the stars? I wondered. Haunting sounds, they bounced off the shouldering slopes of the mountain and into the valley all through the night as the world I thought I knew grew less and less familiar. In the morning, I could find no evidence remaining with which to piece together the nocturnal drama that had unfolded. Dew sparkled brightly off the tips of the meadow grass. The air seemed fresh and innocent, and breathed not a whisper of whatever had transpired in the night. I found myself wondering how many worlds I may have slept through in my life, how many worlds remain invisible to me.

I often find proof of other worlds along the path to the berries: a lifeless vole, its fur wet and licked into an unnatural direction. Or, nearest to the blueberry meadow, another sign: an imprint in the moist earth where midnight hooves sank deep into the mud. Once, a seemingly intact butterfly, its stilled wings stopped mid-beat. What world had it fallen from, I wondered, and what had it risked? What about the snake that skids across the path from one grassy galaxy to the next? Or the watchful world of the deer who grazes by the hedgerow and, when it spots you, bounds away clumsily, with an odd gait? Or the milkweed universe with its flower planets and insect moons, its caterpillar stars that spin and burn until they turn themselves inside out in a supernova of orange wings that flash and flicker all across the great sweep of the meadow?

So many worlds.

Even amongst my own species I find there are places I simply do not know. Yesterday, at the soup kitchen, I sat with a man my own age for whom hunger was his homeland, a place I've never even visited. Another ambassador at the table believed he was a prophet, that he was Saint Paul. His sentences contained familiar words, but I could make no sense of them. All I could do was wonder at his world, offer him another bowl of soup, and feel grateful I do not know the dialect of empty stomach or hear the fiery tongues of hallucination.

The more I pull myself from slumber, the more I realize that the world I know is really a world I *think* I know, that there are boundless realms bouncing against each other continuously. We might get a glimpse into another world when its orbit intersects ours. And who knows how long such meteors might have been traveling to reach us? Ancient photons of distant stars travel millions of years—and through galaxies—before their glimmering light alights upon our cheeks. This celestial phenomenon occurs every moment of the day, whether we are wide-awake or fast asleep. If we're lucky, we might catch the tinsel and flicker of the morning star and feel like something more than the sun rises with the dawn: a chance to see and do things in a new way.

This morning, hiking back with my cache of wild berries, I came around the corner in the path at the same time as a red fox traveling in the opposite direction. Perhaps it too had berry picking in mind, but seeing me, skidded to a stop. For a brief moment we both froze, the borders of our worlds overlapping in the margin. Having come face-to-face so unexpectedly, neither one of us knew quite what to do. Then the elegant creature retreated to a granite out-cropping where it sat looking out over the meadow. The tips of his tawny fur glinted in the morning sunlight, creating a glowing halo effect around his shimmering body. If I had known any russet words of fox I would have spoken them, whispered into his whispery ears, "You are a magnificently beautiful being." But all I could do was wonder at his world as I stood still as stone in the amber glow of foxlight. Indeed, though for the moment my world revolved around his, the fox's fiery red planet spun quietly back out into space as he heard something rustle in the bracken.

His black stockinged paws stepped once, twice into the tall ferns, and he was gone.

Making Hay

ONLY A few days ago the wind rippled over the tops of the grasses, the wispy globes of dandelion and the buttercups, painting great sweeping patterns in the field. But now a more structured design emerges. The stems and leaves and flowers lie in concentric rows that follow the contours of the land, revealing the curvaceous earth from which they sprang. It's the first cut of the season, and everywhere you go this week you can hear the hum and whir of tractors bouncing through hay fields. One day the machines pull the wide-mouthed cutting blade behind their tall wheels; the giant twirling prongs of the hay rake dance behind them the next. The bailers and trucks, with their rickety wooden side rails, follow in turn. If all goes well, that is to say if it does not rain, this tender, sweet first crop of meadow grass will be put up in barns and sheds by week's end.

Like so much of the land here in the northeastern corner of Vermont, our fields are cut by the farmer down the road. Today, one of the hired hands has come by to ted and rake what was freshly mown yesterday. When he sees me he stops the tractor and stills the spinning spokes of the rake, climbs down from the tattered seat, and comes over to say hello. As we shake hands, I feel what must be nearly sixty years of farmwork in the thick skin of his palm. His name, Butch, is embroidered above the pocket of his blue work shirt. They're almost a week late getting out into the fields,

9

he tells me, what with all the rain the last few weeks. But, it'll make for a good crop. He's got to get going though, the other boys will be coming by with the harvester and the truck around noon and it'll take him three times around the field for every one of theirs, don't you know. I want to say, "Reckon so," but I don't. A twinkle starts in Butch's eye and he actually says, "Gotta make hay while the sun shines." It's funny because it's corny, and it's true. Then he's running back to the tractor, scrambling up the tall back wheels and into the bouncy seat like a seventeen-year-old farmboy.

It's too tricky for the big machines to get through the wet swale between the upper and lower meadow, so I keep an opening in this bottom field and a walking path to it cut with a little push mower. In the summer there are wild blueberries ripe for the picking, but year-round it is simply a beautiful, secluded place to walk to. This afternoon, while cutting the grass there, I nicked a low branch of a spruce tree and its spicy smell filled the hot air. I felt like Proust with his fragrant petites madeleines as a memory from my childhood washed over me. Somewhere in my brain the smell of spruce became that of Vicks VapoRub and I could suddenly feel my mother's hand over my heart rubbing the greasy menthol into my chest. I felt unexpectedly taken care of and immensely loved. The hairs went up on the back of my neck and a shiver ran up my spine as I considered the decades that have passed since I last felt her touch.

I pulled myself back to the present, registered the still-running engine of the mower, and finished the path to the berries. But the experience followed me back through the meadow and up to the house. As I sat on the deck looking out at Bear Mountain and Burke in the distance, I could not shake the longing I felt. Melancholy mixed with a tender, sweet memory.

The sudden appearance of a hummingbird quickly altered my thoughts. He was on his way to the ruby bells tinkling over the edge of the flowerpot not three feet away from where I was sitting. Stopping midair and hovering there, his wings whirring out to each side, he looked like a crucifix momentarily suspended in front of me. Surely a celestial being, a seraph; he was a blur of wings. Then, he was off to the business of gathering fuel from the ringing blossoms.

How simple it is to assign the supernatural to hummingbirds, to fit them into some spiritual metaphor. Indeed, with their bright plumage iridescing in the sun, how could they not become emblems of joy? But, the colors that bounce off their feathers are pigments mixed only by our eyes when we add the element of light. And when we do we name them after what they most resemble: rubies, amethysts, topaz jewels. Or, we take note of their enchanting and flickering flight and dub them purple-crowned fairies, violet-tailed sylphs. More often than not, when we think of hummingbirds, it is as delicate, nectar-sipping things, diminutive spirits that spend their time feasting on ambrosia and beauty.

But the little creatures are omnivorous beings. All manner of insects find their way up those slender, delicate-looking bills. And the life we see as devoted to kissing flowers is, in reality, a struggle to stay alive. The tiny birds have voracious hearts and must feed nearly constantly in order to live. Place a hummingbird feeder outside your window and you can watch altruism and generosity fly away: it quickly becomes *territory*. Pity any fool that dares alight on its sweet shores! The dominant hummer will deliver a dazzling sideswipe. In fact, the little hummingbird is the originator of "shock and awe." Blazing warriors, they duel and joust for sustenance. By day's end, the exhausted things have little energy left. At night their rapid-fire hearts slow to a dangerously low rate. Dropping from nearly five hundred beats per minute to as little as thirty-six, the nocturnal gamble becomes whether or not they will have enough energy in the morning to rev their insatiable hearts up to a life-sustaining rhythm. Some never see the dawn.

Those that wake to a new day haven't the time to bother with yesterday—or tomorrow, for that matter. The future is contained for them in each moment's drop of nectar. If their heart is beating, the only question becomes how to spend those heartbeats. And there's only room for one answer. They live fiercely, spending their heartbeats wildly. Making hay while the sun shines.

Preservation

I'M HAUNTED by a pickle.

The kitchen shelves glimmer with jars of home-made preserves after a summer's worth of gardening, harvesting, and putting up. Strawberry and wild blueberry preserves glisten and glow in their glass cases like gemstones. Clove-scented beets glow deep garnet, and the cauliflower sparkles crystalline, bejeweled with tiny, bright-red, and lethally hot Thai peppers. Brandied blackberries await syrupy slides down midwinter bowls of ice cream or late-night waffles. Freshly jarred applesauce spiked with a bit of vanilla cools off after its recent dip in the canner's hot water bath. Zucchini pickles stack up right next to the gingered green beans. Honey dills, bread n' butters, sweet and sours, gherkins, mustard pickles and relishes: everything's here. Everything except the tiny pickles my grandmother used to put up in glass jars with glass lids and rubber seals, the ones she'd set on the wobbly wooden cellar stairs in expectation of family dinners around the old oak table, its wooden length stretched by seemingly innumerable leaves and warmed by the old wood-fired cookstove.

I've spent the summer canning and preserving. Each evening, after a day's worth of picking, peeling, boiling, and packing, I listen attentively for that satisfying pop as the lids expel the last of the air trapped in the jar, creating a safe and long-lasting vacuum, one that will insure garden-picked taste in snow-covered January. But there is no satisfaction when it comes to the itty-bitty sour pickles I'm craving. Always at the table while I was growing up, and now the recipe is long since lost. Cheek suckingly sour and smaller than my childhood fingers, they were a staple of the New England boiled dinners that so often appeared at the table along with sons and daughters, aunts and uncles and cousins. Part of the satisfaction of eating them was the challenge of fishing the little things out of the jar. You might think you had a good hold on one but then, like a shimmering fish, it would slip through your fingers and splash back into the briny depths. But oh, once caught and brought to your lips, it promised something beyond the ordinary. I can still recall the shock of sour at first bite, how the vinegar squirted over my tongue and the exquisite tingling that would dance between my cheeks, making my mouth water with abandon. But try as I might, I cannot seem to duplicate the jolting flavor of my Grandmother's pickles.

If I had known as a child that I'd be craving her pickles now, that I would spend an entire summer trying to find that mysterious combination of snap, sour, and surprise, I would have asked her for the recipe and carefully copied it down in my best childhood penmanship. But I didn't think anything of it then. How could I? I never thought that there might come a day when there would be no pickles lined up on the cellar stairs, or that the old table would no longer groan under the weight of boiled dinners, or that grandmothers, mothers and fathers, aunts and uncles and cousins would disappear one by one from the table.

Still, the tongue remembers, it reminisces: a bite of the past, a spoonful of summer, a taste of home . . . the bottle of vinegar passed with the plate of root vegetables at family gatherings, my mother and her brother fighting over the last of the parsnips. Aunts gathered in the kitchen afterwards, all in their flowery aprons and housecoats, washing the dishes, and the menfolk returning when it was time to run whatever was left of the boiled dinner through the food mill so that, in the morning, there would be red flannel hash for breakfast. And those sure and dependable pickles, small but steadfast, passed round the table at every gathering.

Once they even showed up out in the maple grove at my uncle's sugar shack when the grownups threw a traditional sugar-on-snow party for the kids. Our eyes wide in anticipation and our pant legs frozen stiff from playing in the snow, we watched the thick maple syrup, boiled until it was nearly candy, turn gooey and chewy as it was drizzled over chunks of icy snow. The adults ate theirs with bites of the little pickles in order to cut the sweetness. Like my young cousins, at the time I found the concept of balancing sweet with sour an absurd one. But I was mesmerized by the unexpected appearance of that familiar jar of pickles in the snowy woods.

My partner has his own pickle ghost: half-sours put up in an earthen crock by his Polish aunt and set in the cool basement to ripen and turn. On visits he would paddle quietly downstairs with his brother, and together they would sneak as many of the big dills as their little hands and stomachs could handle. Careful to replace the heavy stoneware plate that held the pickles submerged in brine, the two boys thought they were very clever. Cioci (Auntie) never said a word, but simply kept the crock full with cucumbers picked from her large and well-tended garden. This summer we tried to make Cioci's pickles, too. But had she kept the crock covered with a square of cheesecloth or a heavy lid? Did she leave the stem ends of the cukes intact, as we'd read in some recipes, and shave off a bit from the blossom end? Or include a grape leaf for extra crunch? The memory was mostly about *sneaking* the pickle, not making it.

Our first try was a salty disaster. Another batch seemed to hold some promise but then suddenly turned to mush. Ultimately, after reading dozens of variations on fermenting cucumbers in a crock, we realized we were following steps to make a finished pickle when what we really wanted was something more immediate and clandestine, something forbidden: a pickle that would make our hearts pound as we reached for it.

So we've spent the summer in a pickle, as it were, trying to recapture a pair of lost recipes: the salty crunch of Cioci's half-sours and the compact zing of Gram's little cornichons. The tricky part was that each of us was trying to recapture not just a pickle but a pickled memory. The challenge was how to add to the crock the thrill of sneaking a bite, or stir in the damp, earthy smell of a dirt-floor cellar. Vivid yet elusive, the pickles are no longer preserved in vinegar or salt, but float somewhere in the briny depths between our taste buds and a sleepy neuron dozing quietly in some dusty corner of the brain. Neuroscientists can now tell us that the dusty corner is likely to be somewhere in the hippocampus or amygdala, the parts of the brain that maintain emotions and long-term memory. Whereas all of our other senses travel through different regions of the brain, taste and smell shoot directly to memory.

We persisted. Taste, memory, and emotion seemed to combine with increasing intensity at every bite. Dinner conversations became sassy as each meal was accompanied by a potentially Proustian pickle. We evaluated the nuance and complexity of each new batch as if it were a fine wine. "Initially quite sour, this pickle opens slowly to reveal salty, earthy undertones," one of us might sputter. Or, "A bit plump, but seductive, with a long, steely finish. Impressive nose, peppery, it promises to taste even better in three months." For as long as the garden kept pumping out cucumbers (a brief but precious few weeks here in New England), we became students of the briny, the bitter, and all things biting. We spent hours discerning taut from crisp, and crisp from crunchy, or debating the subtle differences between tart and tangy.

Sour, it turns out, has a split personality. There's the good sour, the one that adds perk and pizzazz to our otherwise bland diet. And then there is sour's evil twin, the one that spoils our food. We refer to bad feelings as sour grapes, and yet we intentionally make other fruits and veggies sour. In fact, we deliberately make any number of foods sour, pickling pig's feet, flower buds, or hard-boiled eggs. Not even the little herring can escape our passion for pucker. Sour milk in the carton is something you don't want to pour into your morning coffee or tea, but how sad the baked potato would become without its luscious slather of sour cream. And home bakers have long practiced the art of clabbering, or souring the milk in a recipe on purpose, to produce a tart flavor and ensure a tender crumb. Whenever she made doughnuts, Gram always soured the milk. Coincidentally, Cioci performed a similar bit of alchemy when she whisked cream into her vinegary beet soup, creating a shockingly pink and velvety borscht. Sour, when we're on its good side, can perform miracles. The pickle, for example: cucumber, plus vinegar, plus salt and spice, somehow adds up to more than the sum of its parts.

The power of sour is something our grandparents must have understood well. Canning, pickling, and preserving were necessary elements of their economy. Food was something to be thought about carefully in a time before there was a grocery store on every corner stocking whatever you might wish for, whether it was in season or not. But I find myself wondering if there might be more to sour than simple preservation, and if women like Gram and Cioci knew what that was. Whatever they put up in those gleaming glass jars, whether brined or vinegared, was not only sustaining but symbolic. It was the present carried into the future: a certain hopefulness, perhaps. Or, maybe they canned as a way of remembering the past. Maybe they understood some secret about how the counterweight of sour makes the sweetness of memory endure.

Gram outlived her husband by decades, having attended to him in his wheelchair for the last years of his life. She stood stoically first by the graveside of her infant child, then her grown son, and finally two of her daughters, one of them my mother. Sometimes I wonder if, when she soured the milk in her doughnut batter, she was thinking of them. As a child, I watched her make those doughnuts any number of times. I would stand on a chair next to the counter and follow her hands as she whipped up a batch from memory. I imagined we were scientists as she stirred a tablespoon of vinegar into the measuring cup of milk and waited for the predictable results. When she would add a pinch of grated nutmeg to the batter, we became explorers returning with fragrant spices from faraway lands. Often, she would hand me the tin cutter and I would stamp out the floppy, concentric circles of dough in preparation for their deep-fry dip in the hot lard. In my mind's eye, I can see her making chocolate cake, cinnamon buns, fresh dough-nuts, oatmeal cookies, even homemade fudge, but I never actually saw her put up those little pickles. They simply and mysteriously appeared on the old cellar stairs. So, I've searched all summer to find the secret ingredient, trying various concoctions of vinegars, incantatory grape leaves, conjuring roots, seeds of hope. I never thought to measure in longing or the understanding of just how short the grow-ing season is, how moments linger for such a short time. Or that some are all too brief and begin to flicker and fade, unless we can somehow preserve them.

Hark

I HEARD the call before I ever saw their slanting silhouettes string across the sky. It began somewhere to the north, beyond the ridge of the meadow, and grew louder, more urgent, more resonant until at last its source became clear. Even though I had stopped to watch and listen to their kin gathering raucously in the cornfield yesterday, I was still surprised first to hear and then to see skein after skein of the wild geese flying over the blueberry barren today, their smoke-grey shoulders pumping the chill morning air. All day their call haunted me as the many flocks feathered aloft, repeating the same blue word over and over, their plaintive song falling like snow onto the valley below. And perhaps because the ground was dappled with its first unexpected snow of the season, and the air and sky looked and felt also like first snow, the birds' anthem seemed that much more plaintive.

I strained to catch what I could of the melody of their flight, sung in that far-feathered language. I considered too who else might have heard the geese and whether they also struggled to translate the call, for the entire meadow seemed suddenly stilled to listen. Did the deer hear? Did the fox listen? Did the goldenrod heed their call and bend like monks low to the ground under their scapulars and hoods of first snow? Did the maples attend and interpret the call into the surrendering fall of their last, lingering leaves?

There were no familiar words to translate in the voices of the birds, and I was reminded of the saying "Half is the song that reaches the ear, and half is the hearing." Whoever coined the phrase, it felt like an apt sentiment in the midst of all this departure and, hopefully, return. I cannot hear the clamorous chorus and not wonder about home, about homecoming. How today their home is somewhere south of here, yet in the spring home will be north again. How do they know to leave home in order to arrive home, and when to leave? How is it that they know how to get there? Or do they? Do they ask for proof of arrival before they lift up from everything they've known in order to arrive at what they hope for? And do they understand the implications of that risk?

The geese are not alone. Billions of their feathered compatriots migrate unerringly between far-flung wintering grounds in the south and nesting grounds that reach just as far north. At any given moment, spring or fall, millions of migrants chart the invisible currents and channels in the air above us, their course engraved on some interior map.

As above, so below. The newt and the frog both embark upon the passage from piney woods to vernal pool, from land to water. The smelt run upstream. Even year-round denizens journey from their winter deeryards and mountain dens and come down into the impossible and suddenly green valley, and back again. The migratory instinct pulls mysteriously.

The pioneers who headed west in hopes of open land and second chances must have known something akin to that force. That yearning to vault beyond the confines of all they had ever known pulled them across an entire continent. What they would find there, wherever *there* was, remained for them unknown until they arrived. Still, beyond each day's horizon there was the presence of possibility. My great-grandfather was among those pioneers, the allure and promise of the Dakota Territories prying him off his Vermont hilltop. New counties were being founded larger than entire eastern states. I try to imagine a young Elmore Isaac peering out over his first glimpse of the place, his eyes squinting into the far sage-filled distance, and thinking, "Yep, fine place to build a nest." Four dollars got him a homestead claim to one hundred sixty acres.

His handiness at stacking sod into sturdy walls caught the attention of a certain young lady, Carrie, whose smile, in turn, proved sweeter than the smell of the sun-warmed prairie. Soon young children were as plentiful around the homestead as sagebrush or the unceasing wind. Their youngest girl, my grandmother Leila, wasn't even five years old when the migratory pull called Carrie and Elmore back home. This time they knew the way and what to expect beyond the horizon, although for Leila and her siblings the journey east was unfamiliar territory: leaving home in order to arrive home.

But then maybe the destination isn't the point. Too often, wanting to be sure of where we're headed simply prevents us from heading anywhere at all. Leila held a pair of moccasins in her lap on that eastward wagon ride home: a gift from a Sioux family that had forever lived on the land that was now being divided up into homesteads by white men, my great-grandfather included. What Native people have always known so well is that the land does not belong to any of us; we belong to it. And the understanding that all directions are holy. Or, as an old friend is fond of quoting, "To be on the way is to be home."

How do we know what cannot be proved? This is always the question. Can we ever fully grasp, for example, the resolve that must exist in the tissue-thin wings of the monarch butterfly as they carry that diminutive creature, weighing less than a gram, over thousands of miles in order to alight upon the flock of wild, white milkweed that gathers at the head of the meadow? Or whether the tall, weathered reeds silently anticipate all winter long the red-winged blackbird's clamorous return? Sure, we witness these comings and goings. But the mechanics of and reason for such translocation is still a mystery. Are we talking about instinct here, or some deep, divine pull? Or might it be belief or even memory? This is where empirical knowledge disappoints. Things not understood are not necessarily unreal. Flocks of memories can appear out of nowhere. Beliefs can migrate; time can fly.

Nothing stands still.

Surely these winged pilgrims must be watched over, must believe themselves that they are watched over by something greater than themselves. They leave, they return with such authority, such certainty—no, not certainty, but ultimate hope. And maybe that is the beckoning word the geese repeat over and over as they slant through the air: hope, a beautiful, strong word, and in their tongue even sweeter than I, being wingless, will ever know. They have no irrefutable proof with which to be certain of their destination. Indeed, many in the flock have never even made the journey. Perhaps what elevates the gliding birds is not physics or truth, but rather a sure belief that there are truths that lay beyond proof.

Faith. It's as much a part of the geese as their wings. They wear it as plumage. Look: it propels them through the sky.

Was, Is, Will Be . . .

A CERTAIN hush has fallen with the snow on the meadow. The summer symphony of birdsong long since flown, the trees and ground blanketed with a muffling fluff of white, the place not only looks but sounds different. The cold air rattles the dry meadow grasses; they rustle and scrape in the wind. Footsteps now crunch where they once padded silently over mossy paths. The naked branches of poplar and birch, cold and brittle in the early winter chill, click and chatter at the slightest breeze. The evergreens don't seem to mind, though: they quietly sway back and forth, each branch cuddled under a quilt of feathery white like a sleeping child.

And written upon the snow, animal tracks strung in long sentences everywhere: turkey scratches like Chinese characters, the amble and bound of a deer. The staccato hop and leap of rabbit marches rhythmically off into the distance, while the rambling, meandering line of fox zags this way and that as nose follows toes. Etched into the silvery white in the palest shade of icy powder blue, the tracks are something left behind. They remain and remind. Embossed evidence, their presence is proof of absence. The flash of deer-tail, the shimmer of bronze feathers are nowhere to be seen. Yet I believe that the deer is still here, that I will come upon the fox again when I least expect to, just as I know and believe there are still wild blueberries carpeting the ground underneath this fresh drift of snow.

Not far from where the now-invisible berries hibernate is an entire pond that *isn't* there. It used to be there, fade-proof and indelible, but in the summer of 1810 it ran away and never came back. Today a stone marker stands on the spot where the waters of Runaway Pond once flowed and explains the mystery of their liquid disappearance: How the millers, wanting greater waters to power their gristmills and sawmills downriver from the pond, dug a wide channel into the shore, not knowing that beneath the pond's edge was nothing but loose sand.

When the channel was completed, the outpouring water quickly began to wash away the earth below it. The sandy soil could not contain the full contents of the pond. The ditch-diggers watched helplessly as the hoped-for mill waters became floodwaters before their very eyes. Out flew the entire lake, a wild flock of waters, trees, boulders and earth, leaving in its wake a landscape forever changed.

Today, when I stand in that landscape I am struck by how Runaway is still so palpably present, yet so distinctly absent at the same time. Without fail, I always look up and try to imagine its waters rising more than a hundred feet above me as I walk along the now-dry lakebed. Where *did* Runaway go? How is it that an entire body of water, some-thing we tend to think of as permanent, eternal—how is it that it could be and then not be?

I was thirteen when my father told me my mother was dying. I remember how his words came tumbling out of his mouth just as he was leaving to work the late shift at the fac-tory two towns over, his blue winter coat already bundled around him, his lunch sack already in his hand. I was making cookies for her. She was in their bedroom down the hall. He grabbed his thermos and left. I continued to stir the batter as tears ran down my cheeks and into the bowl. In the next few months I learned to cook whatever she felt hungry for, chemotherapy having wiped out most of her desire to eat. The ground beneath us, like the sandy shores of Runaway, had already begun to slip away.

Years later, I watched the same disappearing act play out in my father's body. His lungs evaporating, not only did his ability to breathe disappear into thin air, his every breath *became* thin air, a struggle for oxygen. Where once I could barely get my arms around the hard-working, independent, barrel-chested man he was, suddenly I could enfold him entirely in my embrace. The first time I felt his bones through his skin I was surprised, although I should have recognized the landscape. I didn't want to look into some yawning chasm where once moved the shining, beautiful, deep waters of his life.

I don't know how to explain disappearance. The very word itself tells me that I can no longer see something, just as the stone marker tells me I can no longer see the pond. But I do. Even if its sparkling waters have effervesced into something else entirely, the pond still exists somehow in that granite memorial, in our remembering it. I cannot prove this. But doesn't most of what we believe to be true require leap after blind leap into the unverifiable? We believe in the existence of any number of things that cannot be seen. Especially if something is left behind by which to remember them: icy blue tracks in the morning snow, letters carved into stone, a shred of cloth that once touched the body of a beloved, a bit of bone or even some ancient ceremony.

Relics remind: they make memory into meaning.

When medieval pilgrims undertook long, arduous journeys to look upon some splinter of wood or lock of hair, they were not only remembering but also believing. In fact, such reminders were so treasured that they were enshrined in elaborate vessels: reliquaries, ossuaries, bone boxes made of precious gold and encrusted with ivory, enamel, and jewels. Entire cathedrals were built to house such memories. Of course, the one true jawbone of John the Baptist was preserved in any number of chapels, each claiming authenticity. And more than one church claimed the relic of the holy prepuce, the bit left over after Jesus' circumcision. But this intersection of memory and belief is not a question of fact and history, of that which can be corroborated. Nor is it about truth, necessarily, but the kind of big *t* Truth that guides and shapes our hearts and minds.

Who knows why we remember certain things in certain ways? While we might be able to prove that a memory first forms as a changed connection between two neurons, neuroscience is still in awe at the power and intricacies of that relationship. Sometimes memory is a disappearing pond, and sometimes it is more like a carving river that both fits and shapes its banks at once. Our memories create the landscape of our minds, what we believe, and thus our experience of the world. A slippery thing, then, memory: impossible to hold entirely in our hands, never still, its boundaries yielding to the very flow of our relationship to and with it.

The snow melts, the river swells. There are places where the current is swift, where the water bubbles and sparks, and others where it slows or spins lazily in little eddies and coves by the bank. There might be complex twists and turns, complicated oxbows or long stretches of quiet water, but the river moves, is moving. And as it moves the river sweeps away bits of rock and sand from its banks, depositing them downstream in some mysterious, future location yet to be known.

The destination of so many of my own childhood sojourns and adventures was any number of spots along the Twenty-Mile Stream, a short hike from my grandmother's house, where I spent the summers. If you followed the path up the hill and around the town ball field, you would come to a steep set of rocks that tumbled like steps down to the swimming place we all simply called the ten-foot hole. If we were feeling adventurous, we might hike further upstream to the equally unimaginatively named twenty-foot hole, where the "big" kids hung out and did back flips and played "chicken" in the glacially cold water.

Before we made the trek to the stream, though, my sister and I would first walk down the road to the general store, the one business in town, and purchase what we called a picnic but was simply individual Table Talk pies and soda pop. Always coconut cream and root beer for me; what my sister picked out I no longer remember. I do recall a certain picnic at the swimming hole when one of my sister's new sneakers slid in slow motion, just ahead of our grasping hands, down the big rock we were sitting on and into the current of the little brook. We were surprised to see that it did not sink, but drifted away downstream like a boat. We laughed at the thought of her sneaker sailing all the way to the ocean: the sights it would see, the adventures it would have!

Sometimes the whole family would pile into the car for a picnic, although we wouldn't head for the swimming hole but for the country road named after the stream. Along the way we'd listen to our parents reminisce as we passed landmarks from their respective pasts: the little schoolhouse, the cellar hole of the old homestead. Our destination was the family plot at the cemetery, an old New England burial place where haphazard rows of tipsy headstones tumbled up one side of a hill and down the other. In that borderland between presence and absence, Gram would visit her husband's grave and sometimes bend down low over the small headstone of their infant daughter. Mom would adjust the small American flag that fluttered over the bronze plaque of her brother's grave while Dad trimmed the meadow grass with a hand scythe. Afterwards, there might be egg-salad sandwiches, tart tiny pickles, and oatmeal cookies.

How little I understood about memory and our relationship to the past when we buried my mother there next to her family, my younger self standing in that dusty ribbon of road, not entirely sure of what was going on. History isn't simply a record but an ongoing process of revision, our relationship with it evolving over time and through the events of our lives. So many years later, as I stood in that same place to inter my father's ashes next to my mother, the simple, sad notes of the bugle playing taps echoed off the hillside; they hung hauntingly in the air. But before they drifted away I lacquered them with gold and built a chapel for them inside me. I'm not referring here to the gloss of nostalgia or to the irrefutable confinement of fact, but to the living waters of reconsideration.

If we believe with Einstein that space and time are relative and only the speed of light is constant, maybe the river isn't really moving at all. What if the past isn't past but is present somehow in the sum of who we are, in the intersection of memory and belief? From this ramifying perspective, the river branches into any number of ways to understand and interpret memory, to define truth. What would our lives look like if, instead of slogging through space and time, we simply lived at the speed of light? If we could, like T.S. Eliot, figure out that "what might have been and what has been point to one end, which is always present"?

Whenever we stayed at my grandmother's house I always slept in what was known as "the little room." Never meant to be a bedroom, the cozy nook was an angled space carved out under the sloping eaves of the old farmhouse. The ceiling slanted every which way and the only window hung at a curious angle. But inside the little room were two treasures: a small cot-sized featherbed and the door to the attic. I was fascinated with the attic door because it wasn't the usual rectangle, but had instead been cut into a trapezoid in order to fit the crooked alcove at the head of the stairs; perhaps more fascinating was that which lay beyond it: the dusty, curious attic itself. On one visit there, I had found ceramic dolls, the clay figures my mother and her sisters must have played with as children, and had carefully compared them with my plastic action figures. All one piece and all glazed a porcelain white, the childhood relics couldn't move their arms and legs like my Batman figure could. And how did my aunts ever know what shade the doll's eyes were, or the color of their cloaks? But, the object that held my attention more than any other was the old trunk that lurked in the back of the attic. Inside, a tray attached itself to the lid so that as you opened the trunk the tray also lifted up in order to offer a better view of the full contents. The first time my little fingers pried open the lid and the tray started to move, I thought someone—or something—was inside and trying to get out. I was so spooked I slammed the top shut and ran out of the attic.

The featherbed was far from scary. Accustomed to the flat, smooth support of my spring mattress at home, I delighted in the pillowy mushiness of that giant down cushion. The bed fit snugly under the eaves as if the odd space were built especially to house its smooth, rounded iron frame and headboard. I don't remember how it began, but there was a certain ritual that accompanied featherbed nights. Once upstairs and in the little room, my father would lift me up in his arms and hold me out over the puffy bed. Pretending to drop me into the fluff, he'd lift me up and down, chuckling, "One . . . two . . . two-and-a-half . . ." And then I would be falling, sinking down into the down, until only my nose peaked out from its soft, dreamy depths.

"*Again*," I want to say, almost fifty years later, "do it again!"

By the time we'd made our way home from visiting Gram's I would have inevitably fallen asleep on the slick, vinyl back seat of the family's brown, paneled station wagon. I'd stir a bit, suddenly aware of hushed whispers, as my father once again lifted me up in his arms and carried me inside. This would become the scene of my first lie: most times I had, in fact, awoken, but I feigned sleep in order to remain in his arms; to fall once again into the safe warmth of his embrace. Whether he caught on to the charade or not I'll never know. Nor can I say how many times my father carried me in his arms or let me tumble giggling into that downy drift of feathers. But, in my memory, I am often there, falling over and over again into the featherbed in the little room at the head of the stairs.

Blue Moon

YESTERDAY I stopped at the market and was amazed to find a great display of boxed blueberries. I was amazed because it is winter outside and most blueberries, I know, are hibernating under a blanket of snow or waiting in my freezer to be tossed into muffins or morning shakes. After spending the summer with their wild cousins, I wasn't even sure the giant things *were* blueberries. Stacked row upon row, they rested beneath the fluorescent lights after what must have been a very long flight from South America. Since when, I wondered, did blueberries become tropical fruit?

Once, we told time by what was ripe in the garden. Even those who had no land to till could still figure where they were in the year according to the produce heaped and hawked in the market. Tender stalks of asparagus heralded spring and the close of a months-long fast from anything green. Strawberries meant June was frolicking about in the long sunlit days of summer. Apples snapped in the crisp autumn air. When the cucumbers came in, all else ground to a halt so that the little buggers could be packed into crocks and jars and sliced over dinner salads for weeks. Summer days were measured by what berries were ripe, and everyone understood the difference between those succulent first moments of strawberry and the last glowing moments of blueberry, when the little jewels burned incandescent in the late-summer sun. Everyone waited with anticipation for the first bite of sweet corn, some yielding to temptation and wading out into the field to shuck an ear right off the stalk, strip off husk and silk, and bite into those tender, milky sweet kernels.

And as we ate our way through the year we watched the moon grow thin and fat and thin again. We named each month's ripening moon by our guts; the precious days of June sweetened by the Honey Moon, September's bounty guided by the Harvest Moon. The freezing nights and relatively warm days of March were illuminated by the Sap Moon. In May came the Corn-Planting Moon, which became the Green Corn Moon of August. Time ticked to a natural rhythm and frolicked in the waves of squash and plum and wild leek. Day and night, we looked not to our wrists or a dial on the wall, but to the sky above our heads and the earth beneath our feet.

Today our markets overflow with tomatoes in mid-winter. Lemons, green beans, fruits wild and exotic stack up in three-ring circus acts week after week. Protected by supermarket powers, salad greens taunt the northern winds of winter from Anchorage to Boothbay. Pineapples, once a jet-setting rarity in most parts of the United States, now sulk in the aisles as harried shoppers hurry past. They gather occasionally for some fruit group therapy with the coconuts and reminisce about the good ol' times. Gone are the heady days of limited engagements. Today our markets broadcast out of season produce like a gastronomical equivalent of CNN: "All broccoli, all the time." Never mind if a certain sought-after character can't be found anywhere in the coun-try, we simply snatch them unsuspecting from another land and extradite them to the nearest shopping facility.

Spices, too, seem to have lost their panache, or at least become so commonplace that they no longer occupy their former starring role in high seas adventures. Extras now, they're cast row upon row in aisle six or seven. Poor vanilla! We seem to have forgotten its sweet orchid lineage, reducing it to ho-hum status, an emblem of plain. It wasn't that long ago that immigrants chose to pack up poppy seed and down feathers as the most important things to bring with them to their new country, or stitched an envelope of savory saffron threads into the hem of their only garments.

When was the last time we thought of our food as precious? Whatever happened to the delight we used to feel at finding an orange in our holiday stocking? Sure, we go bonkers over blackberries and apples, but only if they're wireless and MP3 compatible. Have we gorged on virtual fruit so long that we've forgotten how to taste real food? So what if we can buy rubbery tomatoes or cardboard peaches in January! Does that really make us any better off than we used to be? Or, does it simply make us numb to what we put into our mouths, robbing us of the juicy gift of anticipation? Something poignant has perished in our pursuit of the imperishable.

We've sacrificed authenticity in the name of progress, bred out nuance in favor of easy shipping. Remember the earthy taste of resurrection in newly sprouted asparagus, or the strange way our mouths would water if it rained, knowing that tomorrow there'd be wild mushroom soup for dinner? Or, the pilgrimage we traveled each time we tasted the first strawberry of the season, the memory crumbs of shortcake and sweet ruby syrup, the creamy goodness of watching each other spoon the luscious stuff into our opened mouths?

Plato attributed the sensation of different tastes to the absorption of flavor into small veins on the tongue, which then carried it to the heart to be tasted. What if he was right and we eat with our hearts?

How I Wonder What You Are

THE SKY was extraordinarily clear last night and I went out to look at it. The stars were shouting their inexhaustible stories across the dark; I listened with astonishment and delight. A mother bear and her cubs ambled through the firmament above me. Heroes journeyed, sisters gathered and danced, a holy cup filled and turned in the night's light-pierced dome. As the gospel of starlight spangled before me, I wondered about the names of stars and the dotted lines we draw between them.

The late autumn night was crisp in anticipation of winter. The fields shone like silver beneath the onyx sky; the grasses, as if cast in pewter, stood tall and shivering in the dark. Standing there in the starlit meadow, I also could not help thinking of the berries sleeping beneath the stars and was reminded of one of my favorite names for them. Not wanting his children to go hungry, the Great Spirit sent wild blueberries as a gift to his people during a period of increasing scarcity and approaching starvation. Upon careful inspection of these heavenly gifts, a single star could be seen stamped upon each little berry, and from that day on the people called them "starberries." Still visible today, the five-pointed star is what remains of the blossoms from which the berries began: their earlier spring calyx and flower, a little bit of heaven beneath our feet.

I simply call the celestial berries "wild blues." Just over the border in Quebec, though, they seem to be a bit more exotic, advertised on the roadsides on hand-painted signs reading "bleuets sauvage." In the field guide I note their listing as early lowbush or dry-land blueberries, but more officially as *Vaccinium vacillans*. Later in the season the common highbush blueberry will ripen, although to some folks these lovers of the damp earth are known simply as "swampberries." I once read in a dusty book of the dangleberry, a blueberry relative so rare that seldom is there a year when there's even "enough for a pudding." One blueberry is sometimes called the velvetleaf, other times the sourtop. The unappetizingly named hairy huckleberry is, thankfully, inedible. If you were Thoreau you would have called them all whortleberries; if you are a botanist, they're all *Vaccinium*.

The taxonomical urge is seemingly irresistible to us humans. We name things. It's how we make sense of the world. And, for the most part, such simple and vague terms as *cloud* or *berry* simply will not suffice. We crave the delineating comfort of *cumulus* or *stratus*, *huckle* or *blue*. "Will it bring rain or snow," we ask, "wind or warmth?" Will it provide sweetness or not? Indeed, quite often it is helpful, perhaps imperative, to be able to communicate the difference between two things. Otherwise you might end up with a mouthful of hairy huckleberries when you were expecting something else entirely.

Sometimes, though, we get carried away and find more than a few names for the identical.

Gazing up at the same scattering of burning suns, some of us see a swan winging its way through the vaulted night; others see a compassing cross. Three stars in a row might be the belt of that stellar hunter Orion, or the tinseled handle of a saucepan. (In South Africa the same three are a trio of sisters.) The little dipper is also a little fisher, a little bear, or even, in some places, a dragon's wing. Depending on where you stand the stars are either mythical heroes or distant suns, precious diamonds or compressed carbon, under pressure and on fire. Or perhaps, as some believe, they are the departed souls of our beloveds.

"The beginning of wisdom," according to one proverb, "is to call things by their right names." Perhaps that's what motivated our inquisitive ancestors when they first cleaved the world into categories such as genus and species. We continue to base our understanding of all living things on their binomial system. There is inherent power in a name: it can describe, define, and measure. We use them to clarify and to pigeonhole, to bring together and to differentiate. It all depends on where we bring down the blade of separation.

In another legend, not only do blueberries fall from the heavens, so do we. Newborn children, according to the tale, are stars come to earth who will return to the sky upon their deaths.

The year I fell to earth, it seems everyone's eyes were turned to the night sky. Sinatra was crooning over a blue moon. In fact, the moon was very in that year. Henry Mancini's *Moon River* wound its way through both the Oscars and the Grammy awards. Everyone gazed up at the stars and admired their sparkling gowns: Sophia Loren, Judy Garland . . . Red Skelton. The radio fairly crackled with news. We listened with stars in our eyes as Soviet cosmonaut Yuri Gagarin became the first person in space. American Alan Shepard was right behind him, and then, well, everyone was talking about the moon. Suddenly the entire universe seemed ours. President Kennedy was inaugurated and a new era, one filled with hopefulness, seemed to rest easily on his shoulders. He had the stars in his eyes, too, and challenged the entire nation to land one of us on the moon before the decade's end.

But just as importantly, in my little universe, Barbie finally got a boyfriend that year: Ken. Not too far in the future I would be sneaking into my sister's room to play with her dolls. Barbie would be there, along with Ken and (remember?) Skipper, Barbie's little sister. In my sister's room they all lived in a slick and very "mod" carrying case, like a strange oval hatbox, glazed the ubiquitous hot pink. What I wouldn't know as I bent the dolls' plastic limbs into miniature mini-skirts and costumed robes, transforming Barbie into Sophia and Ken into Judy, is that the one I twirled joyously through my fingers was my namesake. That a young woman who found herself in a home for unwed mothers, who might or might not have heard Sinatra singing to her, either did or did not look at me as she answered the nurse's question, "Child's name?"

"Ken" she answered. "His name is Kenneth."

It was October 18th, 1961. The nurse who asked my mother my name methodically transcribed the letters into numerical code: baby boy #3331. The black hatch marks noting that it was six in the morning were already beginning to fade. The doctor present at my birth signed the paper in invisible ink. Anything that might identify me or my mother was erased. Like a Polaroid snapshot developing in reverse, we both vanished into the night as the moon silently, slowly slipped from the sky.

It took me almost forty years to finally look for her, the young woman whose name I now know is Rosalie. Forty years to find out that before my new parents named me Thomas, I had not begun my life as a number, as baby boy #3331, but as Kenneth. How odd, a mother and a grown son, strangers, finding out each other's names for the first time. For years I had held on to all the papers my adoptive parents kept. My father had handed them to me in a yellowed envelope, the story of how I came to be their son. In the bundle of papers, hand typed on onion skin, there is the original agreement between my parents and the adoption agency: "If, for any reason whatever during the residence period, we, the adopting parents, shall decide that we do not wish to make this child legally our own, baby boy #3331 may be returned." Two small burn holes pierce the document near my father's signature. Years later, he would tell me that he was so eager to sign the agreement that his hands were shaking, and ashes had fallen from his cigarette.

He told me this during one of our visits to the Veterans Administration Hospital where I brought him for doctor's appointments and prescription refills. Each visit began with the same routine. I would retrieve a wheelchair from the lobby and help him and his oxygen tank into it, then head through the automatic doors to the check-in desk, which was higher than a wheelchair. The nurse there, whom my father could never quite see over the counter, would dutifully replace his name with a number. If we were going for blood work there was no human contact involved at all, we would just take a ticket with a number on it from the dispenser that hung next to the door to the lab. Then we would wait in a waiting room of other numbers for his number to come up. Weeks passed before I made the connection: my father's reduction to a number in the hospital, and my own numerical origins.

That's when I went to the file cabinet I keep next to my desk and pulled out the old envelope.

After re-reading the agreement, I tallied up the receipts for fees paid: two payments of one hundred fifty dollars each for "adoption services," four dollars and fifty cents for probate fees, and a dollar to the city clerk for a certified copy of the birth certificate. This, I would later come to understand, was an amended birth certificate, one that renamed the characters involved in my beginnings. The original was "retained permanently and sealed," according to state regulations, "for 99 years after the date of the adoptee's birth."

A tiny, square, black-and-white photograph tipped out of the bundle and I saw my sister, four years older than I and also adopted, looking directly into the camera. In the picture I'm sitting in her lap and looking to the side, away from the camera, seemingly unable to bear the photo op of now-we-are-a-family: Little what's-his-name junior. But then, tucked into the corner of the yellowed envelope is a smaller one folded oddly, my new mother's handwriting figuring out my new name, Thomas, across the front. Inside I find a tiny curl of my hair, a little bit of tenderness and intimacy I wasn't expecting amidst all this legal paperwork and numbers. A little bit of truth tucked in between secrets.

When I think of "mother," it is Edith whom I think of, the woman who tucked away that lock of my hair. She was kind and thoughtful, and she loved to laugh. We lived for a while in the little village of Reading, where I remember evening walks up a dirt road. My sister and I caught fireflies on one of those walks. When our clenched hands couldn't hold any more blinking bugs, and still others were twinkling like stars all around us, Mom put the beetles in the thin nylon of our jacket pockets and we walked back home glowing and giggling all the way.

But what about Rosalie, especially now that I know her name and that she named me? I've struggled over the years to identify her, to simply refer to her. *Birthmother* just sounds too technical, too biological and legal to define someone who bothered to name the child she knew she would relinquish.

Our parents did not hide the fact from my sister and me that we had been adopted. But as I grew up and heard how other people talked about adoption, I began to realize that not everyone was so open about the topic. This was before Roe v. Wade, and adoption, amongst other topics, was not as freely discussed as it is today. Only later in my life did I come to realize that talking about adoption also meant talking about illegitimacy and infertility. Sex. Secret things. And even though it was clear that my new parents— the only parents I ever really knew—loved me, I could not get my head around that age-old adoption story. There might be variations on the theme, but generation after generation replays the same basic message: we adopted you, we chose you, because we really and truly wanted you, and your other parents just couldn't take care of you. For me, it didn't make much room for why my birthparents couldn't take care of me. Eventually, "couldn't" easily became "didn't want to" in my young head, and I started to insert words like "rejected," "abandoned," and "discarded" into the story.

I did not mention these misnomers to my parents. At some point, I'd convinced myself that if I had been chosen, then if I said the wrong thing or acted the wrong way, the opposite could be true as well:

"If, for any reason whatever during the residence period, we, the adopting parents shall decide that we do not wish to make this child legally our own, baby boy #3331 may be returned…"

This is about answering the question "Who do you think you are?" About figuring out whether that someone is the same today as yesterday, or different. For too many years my name was Afraid-of-You-Rejecting-Me. I thought my name was Not-Good-Enough. I answered to Unworthy. I wasted untold moments as Just-Passing-Through. I wore those words as if they were my name, and thinking they were my name, I believed that's who I was. We believe we *are* who we are called, even if we're the only one doing the calling.

But the name that can be named is not the eternal name. So says the philosopher, at least. The process and importance of naming has been understood by visionaries from every place and time. In our Western civilization the name we are given at birth is usually the same one inscribed upon our tombstone. But in many tribal cultures a person's name is expected to change: one may have a name from birth that is not one's eternal name. In these cultures there are celebrations to declare such new signifiers. The newly named is initiated into his or her more accurate moniker, and the community sees him or her as that new name. The process repeats as necessary. If not, we find ourselves in that telling and ominous line from Rosetti: "My name is Might-have-been: I am also called No-more, Too-late, Farewell."

We know the child by a certain name, but each year choruses proclaim him using other names in Handel's masterpiece, born out of the Prophet Isaiah's words: "For unto us a Child is born, unto us a Son is given . . . and His name shall be called Wonderful." Or think about astonished ol' Sarah, who laughed when Abraham was given the divine promise that she would bear him a son in old age; appropriately, Abraham named the unexpected babe Isaac, meaning "He laughs." Indeed, name claiming is rampant in the Bible: Saul became Paul, Simon became Peter, Sarai became Sarah, Abram became Abraham, Solomon became Jedidiah, and Jacob became Israel, each taking a new name after some turning point in life. This is about acknowledging the mercifully evolutionary aspect of our lives. About helping each other to know and understand that who we are today is not necessarily who we were yesterday or last year or when we were children.

"A name should be taken as an act of liberation, of celebration, of intention," Erica Jong wrote. "A name should be a self-blessing."

It makes sense to categorize and separate berries and clouds. We can hope that stars will remain ever constant. But we do not fit as neatly into such a Latinate world. And naming is not the same as understanding. Who *do* I think I am? A part of baby boy #3331 will always be with me. So will Kenneth and every other blessing I'll ever pull down from the heavens.

Forgetting Fireflies

M Y SISTER doesn't recall our firefly walk. "Fireflies, really?" she asks confusedly. "And I was there? I mean maybe you went for the walk without me." But no, I distinctly remember the both of us giggling and glowing, fireflies alight in our hands, in our pockets; a potent and cherished image from our childhood. Have I distorted the past, then? Or have I just made it up? I wouldn't do that. *Would I?* Or has she forgotten this moment I've carried with me and taken care of ever since we were small? And what about the others who walked with us on that summer night that may or may not have happened? Was our mother there? Was our father? Maybe I caught fireflies all by myself. I have no yellowed photographs with which to prove any of it. All I have is a memory.

If I could provide some flash and click of proof I would show you another scene, this one from the Catskill Game Farm: my sister and I laughing again and pointing to the goat as it stuck its obscene tongue through the fence to pluck a yellow plastic chrysanthemum from our mother's new wicker handbag. She is oblivious to the caprine prank and continues feeding grain to the others at the petting zoo. Our father, having provided for his family penny feed from the gumball machine that dispensed grain instead of candy, would lift the camera, if there had been one, up to his smiling eyes.

Or on a wayside picnic the camera might catch our mother swinging her hand in the air, as if she were already waving goodbye, trying to convince a bee to land elsewhere. Here, her curly locks have been replaced by a thin, straight pixie cut after a grueling round of radiation and chemotherapy. Her children eat fluffernutter sandwiches at the picnic table while her brother and his wife fill water jugs from the cool mountain spring.

Or the picture that flashes across my mind so often, always unbidden: my younger self at my mother's burial standing in the dusty ribbon of the backcountry road that curves around the old family cemetery.

The tattered memory itches at my brain, though, for when I consider the details of it carefully, I cannot say for sure that the road is in fact dirt. Something makes me want to say that maybe the road is paved. So which is it, tar or dirt? I used to know. But the memory is of me standing in the dust and does not feel the same when I picture my feet planted on pavement.

Have I simply invented it all?

Another memory comes to mind. It is the last time I'll see my mother alive, the night she started to have seizures and her friend told my sister to bring me to my room so I wouldn't see. At least I *think* that's what happened. I have forgotten how I got to my room, whether Terri walked me, held me by the hand, or I brought myself there. Was the door locked behind me? Why would I have stayed behind it and not gone to be with my mother? I still hear Carol's voice, the *urgency* of her voice, her yelling muffled by the walls but still audible, "Edith, Edith!" And then to someone (my sister?), "Call the ambulance!"

I am sitting on the edge of my bed and I can hear the sound of the siren far off but coming closer. Then I see the light. At first an amber red glow, it begins to flicker and flame off the tops of the trees, turning them rose and garnet in the night. The ambulance makes its way to the top of the hill and down toward our house, setting everything in its path ablaze. When it turns into our driveway my room ignites in a burst of vivid red. Shards of scarlet light fly around my walls like a crazed flock of cardinals trying to find their way out. I watch from my window as the medics take my mother out of the house and into the ambulance. The crimson lights bounce off the white sheets of the stretcher, off the shiny plastic mask that now covers her nose and mouth. The grass is suddenly a field of poppies; our neighbors' house a ruby. The street glistens burgundy in the night. My heart is beating; everything is beating and flashing red.

Even though that scarlet night has somehow become my last memory of her alive, days passed between the arrival of the ambulance and my mother's final breath. My father brought me to the hospital to see her, although by then she was already lost to us, the morphine drip providing what my father feared and yet desired most for her: an end to the pain, a peaceful rest. I watched her breathe but could not find my mother in that hospital bed; she was no longer the woman I remembered. And yet I was also too young, too naïve to have thought to memorize her: the sound of her laughter, the shape of her smile, the way she tucked her feet beneath her as she settled into her weekly crossword puzzle.

Memories feel solid and real; they give our lives shape. Link them together and you get the story of where you've come from and who you have become. But we can remember a past rosier than it was or let some small detail loom larger than all the rest. We can embroider, embellish, simplify, exaggerate, or rationalize. There are memories we long to excavate and others we would much rather bury away. The trick is that memory takes you wherever it decides to go and not the other way around; that the past is just as fickle as the future and truth is never absolute.

If we are our memories, though, what happens to us when we do forget? Who are we without our stories?

Some things are meant to be forgotten. Thankfully, we do not need to remember how to breathe or the heart's steady rhythm of systole and diastole. Indeed, forgetting is probably as important as remembering in maintaining a sound mind and body. The opposite of forgetting would mean total recall: a memory like a steel trap. How quickly our brains would become overwhelmed. The constant awareness of every cumulative detail, every bit of sensory information whether trivial or important, every event, every shopping list, every word, sound, smell, taste and feeling clamping down on our bloodied legs as we howled to be freed from its inexhaustible iron jaws.

But then what about those bits of information we do not want to forget but do forget? Or the fact that two people can remember the same evening in two completely different ways? What if beauty isn't the only thing in the beholder's eye? Memory, it seems, can be as inherently false as it is intrinsically true. Yet think of the metaphors we fit memory into, and most imply unfailing accuracy: the photograph, the encyclopedia, the filing cabinet. Maybe we create such distinct images of our brains because we dare not acknowledge the sheer and random chaos coiled within that cranial cave of ever-diminishing cells and neurons balanced precariously atop our spine. We might wish for an internal hard drive but more often than not our memory is a sieve.

We are our memories, and yet they fail us.

Once, near the end of his life, my father did not recognize my voice. I'd called before I left the house to see if he wanted me to bring him anything. "Is my son there?" He kept saying, "Let me speak to my son." "It *is* me, Dad, this is your son," I had to say more than once, hoping each time to hear some wisp of recognition in his voice. Was he just confused? Did he really not know who I was? Had he momentarily forgotten who he was talking to, or had he forgotten *me*?

For the last few weeks of his life I spent every day with my father. Each morning I spoke to the nurse who helped take care of him to find out how his night had been. I remember distinctly her kind green eyes. I remember the evening before he died. I had said good night to him and before leaving his room turned to look at him once more from the doorway. I sensed and understood it might be my last sight of him alive. I made my way down the hall to the elevator, pressed the down arrow, and waited for the doors to slide open. As I stood there, an elderly woman in a wheelchair rolled over to me and said plaintively, "Would you call my family? They don't know I'm here; they haven't been here to see me. Nobody comes to see me." With my composure cracking and yet another forgotten soul wheeling toward me, I pressed the down arrow desperately a dozen more times. That's when the nurse with the emerald eyes came around the corner and said to the others behind the nurses' station, "Hasn't anyone told him that the elevator is out of order?"

It wasn't at all funny, but I laughed out loud anyway.

I called that caring woman by her name every day for weeks. Karen? Debby? You would think I could remember her name.

Where do our memories go when they fade away? If something is forgotten, does it cease to exist? Or do our forgotten memories live on somewhere, albeit stranded and unapproachable in some dusty corner of our brains? Perhaps not knowing that you have forgotten is a blessing in disguise. For knowing that I cannot remember the nurse's name or whether that iconic road of my childhood was paved or not feels more like a curse. And what to do about those fireflies? Either my sister has forgotten them, and all I thought the evening meant to us, or I've created a false memory. Whether the former or the latter, I'm not content with either explanation. For when I close my eyes I still see the two of us walking up the road with our parents.

Perhaps a memory can fade away in the space between two neurons and yet still flicker warmly in the chambers of the heart. It is summer and there are fireflies.

On the Way

INTERLACED BETWEEN the wild grasses, the goldenrod licks the meadow with its bright flames. All summer, where the fields never see the hay blade or rake, the sweet timothy and rush-grass stretch their stems toward the sapphire sky. The slender spikes of their seed heads arc and sway in the slightest breeze. By late August their bodies have been bleached the color of shore sand by the sun, and when they sing their oceanic song in the wind I imagine they anchor not a mountain meadow but some sea dune.

The birds remind me where I truly tread. They land sure footedly on the waving spires, their weight bending each one low to the ground. Little brown females—finches, phoebes, and sparrows—they all take turns balancing on the thin lines as if performing a high wire act, inching their tiny bodies up to the tantalizing tips. Over and over they head determinedly to the delectable seed heads, and each time their small weight causes the stems to dip in a graceful, slow-motion curve down to the earth. Every once in a while, when gravity is on their side or when one stalk catches up another, the little seed-eaters reach their delectable destination and delight in the bounty.

I suppose I could wade out into the sea of grasses that splash at the edge of the meadow, but I am content to hold their rosy shell up to my ear and listen to their ebb and flow as I walk around them down the path that leads to the berries. The biggest, ripest, juiciest ones are seldom right along the path, though, so I often venture off the trail into the foot-tripping tangle of low-growing berries and scrub grass. Having left the path, I seldom find that untouched utopia for which I search but, more often than not, come upon another's trail.

Deer runs crisscross these fields. Lift a low branch to snag a perfectly blue berry and suddenly a whole network of mouse trails comes into view. The thin winding course of snake slithers through the grasses in exactly the same place where its ancestors also slid by. In the middle of the barren, the scrub and berry plants might be trodden down in a wide nest where the black bear bedded down that afternoon to paw mouthfuls of berry, leaf, and twig into its autumn-hungry belly.

Beyond these paths I see there are others I cannot see. If the humble bee leaves any trace of its journey as it travels through the meadow, its flight plan shows up nowhere on my radar screen. The little birds fly in on some route known only to them. If the dog is with me she sees newly worn passages with her nose and follows them happily off into the hemlocks. The ruffed grouse seems to have no path at all, only to burst out from the scrub grass in a sudden riot of wings when I least expect it. Sometimes, in a similar flash of surprise, I catch the flick of a white tail as a deer bounds off into the woods.

While deer may have blazed a certain trail through the tall grass, they are not the only ones to use their well-worn course. Most deer runs become interspecies highways traversing the blueberry nation. Other trails, however, reveal a relatively smooth surface, undisturbed by the passage of so many hooves, and whisper the wayfaring way of some padded paw. Or, you might notice the difference in browse along a pathway and look carefully at the nibbled tips of the branches to identify the nibbling passerby. Deer, having incisors only on their bottom jaw, tug and tear at the branches rather than cut through them cleanly, as a rabbit might. I may maintain one way to the berry trove but there are a slew of others that aim for the same delectable spot.

There are so many paths to follow throughout life; some smoother, some choppier. And some you have to blaze all on your own. That's what I was thinking about as I came around the bend in the new path I cleared yesterday, connecting hemlock grove with lower meadow, to find it already scattered with dozens of last night's cordate hoofprints, each cloven track a perfectly holy heart pressed softly into the vesperine earth.

I looked out over that heart-strewn way for several moments, and then stepped quietly onto the path.

Bee Leaving

IN THE beginning there were bees, lots of them. Over the millennia they evolved intricate and exact methods for extracting nectar and pollen from the flowers upon which they depended in order to live. In the process of gathering their sustenance, they inadvertently pollinated flower after flower of plants that then bore the grains, roots, and fruits that *we* depended upon. As they did in the beginning, so do they now: thanks be to bees, indeed.

What's more, bees do not appear to see the lines we draw between the cultivated and the wild. They fly gratefully to both fruit tree and dandelion, berry bush and goldenrod, for their goal is not pollination but something far sweeter. Hovering above a blossoming plant, the forager bee lands and searches out the flower's nectary, where she sucks and feeds, adding converting enzymes that begin the nectar's transformation into what we know as honey. She collects the nectar in a portion of her abdomen called the honey sack. When it is full she returns to her colony where, in the enclosure of the hive, she passes the wild harvest to other worker bees within. The nectar is passed along, bee to bee, the precious sweetness becoming more and more concentrated as it goes.

The insects are capable of converting the nectar into wax, as well, from which they build cells of combs to store this sustaining liquid. After assimilating the sugars from the nectar into their bodies, they secrete small plates of wax through a special gland near their abdomen. Then, using specialized mouth parts, the wax is kneaded until it is ready to mold into the elegant architecture of honeycomb.

At a certain point in time, beeswax was as highly valued as the honey it encased. In the Middle Ages, members of a lord's household could expect to be paid in candles as well as coin. And glad they would have been to receive such sweet light! The pure, clean-burning flame of beeswax would have provided a welcome relief from the smoke and sputter of the more common torch of fat-soaked rags. Surely the night tapers' honeyed scent must have lightened the spirits of our forbears even as it illuminated their dark homes. On Sabbaths and feast days, temples, chapels, and cathedrals consumed the candles voraciously. In fact, for some believers, the candle became a shining metaphor, its light a symbol of the awakened soul. The wax, as pure and chaste as its manifesting bees, was emblematic of a body unstained by sin, while the wick embodied the soul. The candle's flame stood for divinity itself, a mystical being of light. Then we discovered whale oil, then paraffin, then electricity. The light of the hive sputtered, flickered, and all but went out.

Honey, too, was considered a powerful symbol by the ancients, embodying for some purity, for others, wisdom. The Babylonians and Assyrians poured honey on the foundation-stones of their temples. Honey is still used widely in Hinduism as an offering to God. In Jewish tradition, honey is an integral part of Rosh Hashana, the celebration of the Jewish new year, where at the traditional meal, apple slices dipped in honey are eaten to bring about and embody sweet days to come. In Islam, an entire Surah, or section, of the Qur'an is known as an-Nahl, or the Honey Bee: "And thy Lord taught the bee to build its cells in hills, on trees, and in (mankind's) habitations . . . there issues from within their bodies a drink of varying colors, wherein is healing for mankind: verily in this is a Sign for those who give thought."

If we are to believe the New Testament, John the Baptist lived on the golden liquid. Early Christian neophytes were given milk and honey just after their baptism, perhaps in a nod to that elusive land promised over and over again in the Old Testament. Saint Jerome alludes to this cup of milk and honey among other "unsanctioned rites," although by the end of the sixth century the church had put its foot down and had done away completely with the practice.

When I consider carefully the pantry of my childhood I cannot remember a single amber jar of honey ever glistening on our kitchen shelves. And yet I have a distinctly sweet memory from my grade school days: my first taste of that sweet stickiness. On certain days of the week, when my mother worked late at the factory in town, I would hop off the school bus, skip by our long, low ranch house, and schlep over to my classmate Saul's split-level home one street over. Saul's grandmother lived with his family for part of the year, which was not unlike the living situation in my home. While Saul was my age, his sister Naomi sat nearby my sister in their high school classroom. I don't think we ever talked much about what was similar between our two homes and what was different, but I still recall the warm, spicy fragrance of his front hallway, and my fascination with their Old Testament names. I knew that while we went to "church," they went to "temple," but I didn't really understand the difference, or that there should even be one, for that matter.

It was on one of those after school visits that I had my first furtive taste of honey. Saul's ever-aproned grandmother would meet us at their door, cooing mellifluously in some language I didn't know but somehow understood as she embraced first her grandson and then me. Then it was off to the kitchen to prepare a little nosh for her boys. I don't remember what else was going into the bowl that afternoon, but upon seeing the jar of honey, I curiously asked about it and confessed I had never tasted the thick amber liquid. What should a shmuck like me know from honey? My kin, after all, were from the mountains and sweetened their food by the sap of trees. Before I knew what was happening, Saul's grandmother had stuck her finger, glazed with a gob of the goo, into my gaping, goyish mouth.

The thrumming life of the hive is a collective one. Bees, like us, are mostly social creatures. They depend upon each other. A solitary bee could never pollinate every waxy white bell of blueberry blossom or construct the exquisite geometry of honeycomb. But together they create a society sweet with the nectar of cooperation. And it is this attitude of collaboration—this bee attitude—that is the central mystery of every hive. The individual can only be fully understood within the context of the collective whole. The success of the hive depends entirely on how well each resident gets along with the rest.

Bees have long bedazzled and bewitched, capturing our fascination and bedeviling our dreams. Take, for instance, Yeats's hope to "arise and go" to Innisfree, the isle in Lough Gill that he longed to inhabit, where he would build a cabin "of clay and wattles made," and tend to "a hive for the honey-bee, and live alone in the bee-loud glade." Or the sweet hum of Tennyson's dream where "the murmuring of innumerable bees" reverberates through time. Or those brief and breathless lines from New England's beloved daughter: "To make a prairie it takes a clover and one bee, / One clover, and a bee. / And revery. / The revery alone will do, / If bees are few."

I hope Miss Emily is right, because it looks like we might have to rely upon "revery alone." The bees do indeed seem to be few these days: in fact, fewer and fewer each year. While Vermont's honeybees seem to have avoided, to some extent, the disappearance and devastation that Colony Collapse Disorder has brought to hives around the globe, the region's bumblebee population hasn't fared as well. According to the state's ecologist, bumblebees used commercially to pollinate greenhouse crops have infected our native bees with a European parasite. This is not good news for the wild blueberries. Out of some twenty bumble-bee species in Vermont, three have been imperiled by the tiny parasite: one appears to have rebounded, the other two have disappeared. Gone. What's more troubling are the two additional species of bumblebees that are also in decline statewide for reasons nobody can figure out.

There used to be so many of them. Over the years, disease has always played its predictable part, leaving behind its dead for all to try to make sense of. But now they're simply disappearing. It is believed that the vanished, the missing ones, die far from home, and alone.

The reason for the mysterious disappearance has scientists bumbling. Experts around the planet have designed experiments, run tests, and analyzed data. The humble bees are missing in America. They're missing in Brazil, and they're missing in Canada. A number of countries have joined forces and have formed research groups to study the problem. Perhaps it is an unknown bacterium that causes the abrupt departure? Many continue to theorize about parasites or viruses. The climate is changing—what about global warming? What about our penchant for pavement? Maybe the insects have left in a huff after watching us "develop" one too many of their beloved hedgerows and wild pastures into more manicured subdivisions. Or perhaps the pesticides we spray on our crops have somehow turned the bees off, attacked their immune systems, or affected their learning abilities? Researchers have discovered that the winged ones refuse to fly near mobile phones. The ubiquitous devices may be wireless, but of course require a whole network of far-reaching receivers, soaring towers, and circling satellites. What if our constant chatter radiating and buzzing through the atmosphere throws off their navigation systems, and so prevents them from finding their way home?

What about our words?

It seems that the bees vanishing all around us are not only of the striped and winged variety; they are patterns of thinking and action, as well. Just open the newspaper or listen to the day's news and there is plenty of proof that both sweetness and light are disappearing as mysteriously as the blessed bee. I don't understand what has become of us. We used to be thankful, we used to be compassionate. Whatever happened to forgiveness? To mercy?

It used to be so easy for us to see both sweetness and light.

Before and After

THE ROOM is dark; the shades in the windows are pulled down. The place is quiet except for the constant hum and whir of a small fan that spins inside the projector. The carousel advances with a sudden motorized click. An image of a small boy is thrown up onto the blank wall that now serves as a makeshift screen. Eyes focus. The boy wears a thick sweater and tiny baseball cap and is held in the arms of a middle-aged man. The man must be the boy's father. See how he kneels down on the freshly cut grass by the child, one arm wrapped protectively around him, the other holding still a new toy pedal car, a festive bow tied around its steering wheel, its gleaming fenders shining in the day's bright sun. A present. Is it the boy's birthday? Surely it must be. Look how the man smiles at the camera, how the boy gazes up at the man who holds both him and the fantastic red racer in his arms. The man appears to be staring directly at the camera, at us, but it is just as valid to assume he is also looking at the woman who holds the instrument up to her eyes, who smiles as she says "smile" before releasing the shutter.

Hush, but for the quiet spin of the fan.

Click: and the image disappears.

They made a family the only way they knew how. I can't imagine what my life would have been had they not appeared on the front steps of the Elizabeth Lund Home for unwed mothers one day in 1962. They already knew the way to Miss Sybil Howe's office, having met with the adoption worker earlier when they came for the little girl who would become my older sister. I try to imagine our arrival: first my sister Terri, then me. The neighbors never saw our mother expecting, there weren't any of the usual labor or birth pains. We simply appeared. Like the ghostly, developing images of a Polaroid snapshot.

Photographs from that time reveal no trace of our unique origins: we appear every bit the family. Look, there I am in my father's arms with my first toy car. And there, with my new sister at the house where my mother herself grew up. Giddy vacation shots from the Catskill Mountains, Niagara Falls, or Montreal: proof, but proof of what?

I know the parts fixed in the evocative emulsion of photography, the bits immediately after the flash and click of camera lens and bulb. I can hold them in my hands, feel their weight and worth, turn them over and see the familiar scrawl of my mother's handwriting documenting the moment: *Mother holding Tommy, taken at home, 1962.* But what about the before, and the in-between, when the camera was not poised? Surely it wasn't all smiles before my sister and I developed our way into our parents' lives. They'd been married for over a dozen years before they first walked up those stairs to the adoption worker's office.

Sometime in 1952, nearly eight years after their marriage, my parents would pose for a reunion photograph in front of the family farmhouse. My mother's parents sit in the middle of the clan, surrounded by their children and their children's children, the youngest grandchild swaddled and held in grandmother's arms. True to form, my mother has painstakingly identified on the back of the snapshot every subject, all of her siblings and, row by row, their offspring. Aside from her younger, unmarried sister, she is the only sibling yet to have children.

That was more than half a century ago, when a pin-prick of light shot through a swath of darkness documented a single, fleeting moment in time that I can now, unbeliev-ably, hold in my hands. It appears to be an unmediated record, every detail legible and fixed and ready to be in-terrogated, pored over. The lace curtains in the window of the house, the grain of the building's shingles, grandfather's striped suspenders and wondering, nostalgic expression, the crisp crease straight down the legs of Uncle Frank's trousers, the gravel driveway in the foreground, a spruce tree in the distance, and my mother's familiar smile. But it isn't the laughing smile I remember her by, and given the situation, I cannot help thinking that I have discovered that missing picture of my mother expecting.

How I wish I could ask her now what I was too young to know to ask her then. What was it like for her before she married my father or before he left soon after for the war? What was it like after he returned? What about before the steps to the home for unwed mothers, and what about after? I have plenty of photographs and album pages, but the moments they reveal are always elsewhere, never really present or fully past: a having-been inevitably tinted by now's constant revision of memory's then. Still, my mother's smile beckons from each one, even those I conjure up from memory when I close my eyes and think of her. Below her class photo in her senior yearbook is the motto "Happy go lucky, easy go free, nothing on earth bothers me," to which her classmates added, "She is always happy and if there's a dance on, she'll be there."

Her bright, buoyant spirit continues to shine when I read her notations on the reverse of those old family snapshots. Her sister-in-law in nightgown and cap: *Bertha at home with no teeth.* Her younger sister in a mock dipping embrace with my father: *Dorothy and Ray: grounds for divorce!* A picture of my sister and me walking down the road: *Terri and Tommy running away.* Another shows her standing in the front room of Gram's old farmhouse in a new pantsuit the color of spring daffodils and wearing a post-chemo wig. There's no handwriting on the back of this one but I know the story all too well.

The more time I spend looking at these various transcripts of light, with all their photographic requisites of having happened, the more questions they seem to raise. They do not provide proof of anything; they document nothing except the momentary capture of a single moment. It is a mistake to consider them evidence, to assume that photographic detail is the same as the whole story. A stranger looking at the picture of my daffodil-draped mother would know very little from that snapshot about the diagnosis of before, the prognosis of after. Or that the laughing family posed by the front gate of the World's Fair in Montreal was cobbled together from visits to a home for unwed mothers.

I have no snapshots of my birthmother at all to ponder over in these afteryears. What must it have been like for Rosalie, I wonder, before the steps of the home for unwed mothers, before the pains of labor and relinquishment? Before Roe v. Wade? Before everything?

And what about after?

Among the papers that I have been able to acquire from the state, I've found one that lists Rosalie's wishes for her relinquished child. Either she or Miss Sybil has penned the words *a Catholic family with other children* . . . I flip through my stack of before-and-afters and find one of my younger self at my first communion standing with Sister Mary outside of the church, my hands prayerfully clasping my new Sunday Missal. If I could, I would send Rosalie the little square snapshot as proof of . . . What? That she made the right decision? That Miss Sybil made the right choice? I wonder if my birthmother could even look at that square image and think, or perhaps say, "That's my boy?" *Would* she?

Should she?

The first photographs were taken in service to science. Tinkerers of silvers and salts discovered light's secret: that light traced everything in its path from its helium source in the burning sun to its final resting place upon the earth. It carried images. Given the proper combination of focusing lenses and chemical grounds, those images could be unloosed from light, and fixed. Scientists all but abandoned observation, with all its human fallibility, and embraced the scrutiny that only light could etch, and archives of sun drawings amassed, illustrating the fine differences between species of fern or berry or shell.

Human beings are born truth-seekers. The trouble is we've somehow conflated fact and truth. To say that the opposite of truth is falsity does not take into consideration what lies beyond truth, which is knowledge, and beyond that, mystery. The photograph, no matter how finely detailed, can never equal the subject itself, can never fully reveal the complexity of the moments before and after the flash of light that etched it into history. There are finite facts, and there are also infinite realms that float beyond reason and proof.

If I look at the family reunion photograph searching for such proof, for facts, then the lace curtains, the grain of the farmhouse's shingled siding, my uncle's precisely creased pant leg become nothing more than static details. But when I search the picture for truth, for meaning, an ever-unfolding story begins to unfurl and develop.

The matriarch, Leila, who sits surrounded by her family, will outlive her husband and three of her children that now stand around her in the photograph. She looks every bit the Vermont farmwife in her simple housecoat and weary expression. But long before I ever came into the picture, she spent her childhood in the great hills of South Dakota and lived amongst the Sioux. I don't know why her family ever left the Black Hills, but it's easy to imagine that when her father, Elmore Isaac—born not far from the very farmhouse evident in the photograph—grew homesick, he packed up his clan and made the long journey back to the fir-dark slopes of his beloved Green Mountains. Leila would meet the man sitting next to her there, and together they would start a family of their own, eking out a hardscrabble living from a tatter of land torn from those wooded hills.

She always planted beans with corn and squash in her garden so that the vines would climb up the cornstalks, something I now know as a Native American custom often referred to as "the three sisters." She said the fat, prickly squash leaves helped keep the deer away from the garden's sweet morsels. Nevertheless, after Gramps died, we'd sit on the glider out on the porch, evenings, just to catch a glimpse of those majestic, graceful creatures appear out of the misty dusk and partake of her garden's lush and tempting greenery.

I doubt she ever knew the factual basis upholding the three sisters: the beans helping to fix nitrogen in the soil, making the corn and squash roots healthy and strong; the corn stalks providing support for the rambling beans; and the wide squash leaves shading and cooling the soil, slowing evaporation in the summer sun. I prefer to think that she kept this tradition because it reminded her of her childhood on the Great Plains. Some nights, after we'd watched the deer, she'd take out and open the wooden box where she kept the beautifully beaded pair of moccasins she had held on to so lovingly as a young girl during the long wagon ride "back east."

Her second youngest daughter Edith, pictured second from the left in the family photo, married right out of high school. Her young husband left for the war soon after and served aboard an army transport ship that ultimately ran aground in Japan. Throughout the war he would write letters home as well as to his twin brother who had enlisted in the navy. For years after the war, the two brothers would argue over who had put in the most sea time: the soldier or the sailor. But their wartime letters gave no hint of lightheartedness and were full of notes such as "will see you soon—I hope" and "all kidding aside, when I get home war is the last thing that I want to talk about."

When the Western Union telegram arrived, Edith was relieved to read its three-word message: "Am coming home." They would move around for several years after the war, picking destinations by closing their eyes and sticking a pin into a map of the United States. They had eagerly made the trip back to Vermont for the family reunion, making their way in their trusty 1949 Plymouth Coupe. Edith took care to record those who were there, noting that it was her sister's sixth child swaddled in their mother's arms. Her siblings had also arrived in their own basic black Plymouths or sturdy Chevy farm trucks, all except Henry, who rolled up all the way from Virginia in a snappy new Studebaker. The gleaming fleet of Fleetmasters, Town Sedans, and Land Cruisers were lined up side by side, their chrome grills grinning wide, and a photograph was taken for posterity. On the back of the snapshot my mother recorded which car belonged to which family member and the make and year of each vehicle as if they were family members themselves.

It would be almost another decade before Edith would pen the inscription *Mother holding Tommy, taken at home, 1962* on the reverse of the black-and-white image I found in the box of photographs my father had saved. They had returned to Vermont and, after years of trying to have children, contacted the adoption agency up in Burlington. First a girl: Terri Ann. Then, a boy. There was a surprise for him when they brought him home. Edith had tied a ribbon around the steering wheel of the toy car earlier that day. "Smile, hon," she said and, looking through the viewfinder of the camera, watched tenderly as Ray put his arm around the boy who was now their son.

If Heaven Is

HE APPEARED like a flash of azure and turquoise shining out from the edge of the dark woods. Not illuminated but luminous, as if he himself were source of tinsel and flare come down from the exquisite sky incandescent, radiant, incarnate. He flickered in the shadows of the pine and hemlocks like a sapphire jewel and then vanished as quickly as he had appeared.

Later, after a quick check of the field guide confirmed my vision, I read that indigo buntings are not really blue at all, but black, which left me wondering about light, about how the diffraction of the day's brilliance as it shines through the structure of feathers can create color. How optic nerve and retina had transformed the spectral rays of light into the jewel-toned color I thought I saw. How the luminous blue took flight not somewhere in front of me but somewhere inside me: a filament of my imagination.

The experience left me wondering about witness, about proof, and about belief. I know what I saw: a breathtakingly blue bird. Of that I am certain. But if I am to believe the laws of physics, and the bird's feathers are truly black, the question is, where did all that blue come from, and why? The question followed me out into the meadow where I found myself beneath a blueberry sky. And I wondered whether the sky was, in fact, really blue. If a bird can trick the eye, why not the sky?

Most of us have probably known the sky to be blue more often than not, and so the question "Is the sky really blue?" likely sounds absurd to our jaded ears. "The sky has always been blue, that's what color the sky is," we say. The scientific amongst us might point to Sir Isaac Newton and his experiments with crystal prisms that divided light into the rainbowed rays of what we now know as the spectrum. Thus the sky appears blue because, while each of those tinted rays of light has its own particular wavelength or frequency, the shorter blue waves of light are more widely scattered by air molecules and, therefore, our eyes perceive blue when looking at the sky.

Is color molecular, then, or is it imaginary? Do we perceive it with our eyes or make it up somewhere in our minds?

My earliest blue memories reach not skyward, but deep into the inky, indigo waters of mountain lakes from summers long past. Oblivious to the chill of those pine-shaded shores, we'd spend what seemed like hours swimming and splashing until our mothers called us out, concerned over our suddenly ghostly blue lips or shivering limbs. But strangely, unlike our appendages, the rivers and streams that fed those liquid bodies never seemed blue at all. In fact, the swimming hole I'd hike to most often—a shallow basin below the rambling waterfalls of the village brook—is, in memory, sparklingly clear and colorless. Below my feet I could look all the way down through those diamond waters and see the rocky bottom of the mountain streambed.

In my childhood box of crayons there was one in particular that captured my attention more than all the others. Its paper wrapper dubbed it "sea green," but it was the most wonderful shade of aqua that teetered curiously on the edge of blue somewhere between water and sky, porcelain and opal. I had seen the ocean once or twice as a child, vacationing along the New England coastline, and it never looked anything like that one crayon. I spent days dreaming on the cool linoleum floor with that funny stick of blue-green wax. Surely water could never look that color. But the possibility fascinated me. It became my favorite shade. My coloring books became a meditation on sea green: Wilma Flintstone would go to the hairstylist and return with her hair tinted the hue of some ocean that existed only in my mind.

Much later I would finally find that haunting color off the shores of a faraway island and immerse myself in its long-imagined blue come true. Yet, cupped in my hands, that turquoise sea became as clear and colorless as the remembered waters of my childhood brooks and streams.

To quote that colorful character Oscar Wilde: "The true mystery of the world is the visible, not the invisible."

It seems color is as fugitive as time or memory. Sure, we can be certain we see a cobalt creature or a sky-blue sea. But we can never know beyond a doubt whether that which seems to us a certain hue is really that color. Everything we see is an interpretation of light filtered through our eyes, our memories, and our experiences. In other words, the sky blows blue because we blue it. We find comfort in blue skies and associate them with good times. Even in more troubling moments, we often turn to the same sapphire space for salvation. We imagine an azure elsewhere beyond all we can see and populate it with a host of angels and saints and our dearly departed.

Still, even if we'd prefer the sky to be blue more often than not, there are all those other rays of the spectrum hurtling toward us surreptitiously from the heavens. There is red in blue and there is yellow in blue, and blue in red and yellow. I have seen the sky turn an eerie grey-green before a summer storm. And in the gloaming, at a certain moment, the sky will often glow a bewildering orange that somehow paints the far-off mountains a dusky violet.

Painters have long understood this idea of observed color. Awestruck, Delacroix recorded with delight in his journal that the shadows he saw in Africa were not grey or black, but purple. Monet would abandon a painting after a certain amount of time had passed, as the light had changed and thus so had the scene, the moment. Before he went mad, van Gogh must have understood this lesson in light, in how we see. His canvases began to fill up with sea-green skies and wild color combinations of saffron and indigo, crimson and turquoise. Where something called for green, he placed a stroke of cadmium yellow next to one of Prussian blue, letting our eyes, our minds, our hearts mix them into the verdant being of leaf or grass.

Blue feathers, blue waters, blue sky . . . we assign colors to birds and elements and what we most yearn for, hoping to turn the ineffable into something indelible. The sky is blue because that's what color the sky is, we believe. We are certain of it because we have gathered all the tinted evidence we need with our very eyes. We see what we want to see. But if all we really see is light, and individual color is something interpreted, perceived and not seen, is seeing really believing?

And if not, then what do I make of this morning's small, blue miracle shining out from the pinewoods?

Blueberry Fool

THE BERRIES are gone, their blueness incandescent only in memory now. Even though it is still officially summer, the first tinge of autumn already russets their leaves. Before long they will be but a remembered presence as they disappear completely beneath winter's deep blanket. I miss them in anticipation and do not want to see them go. I miss heading out into the bird-sung morning to sit in the grasses and pick the sweet blue pearls. I miss how the repetitive sounds and movements of berry falling into bucket would transfix, and the ensuing, predictable fall into a daydreaming that echoed with memory's deep song. I miss the spectral chorus of the insects, invisible to me in the tangle of meadow grass, as they clicked and whirred in their own universe. How kneeling there in the summer ripe meadow, the world felt right, and I thought I might have caught a glimpse of paradise.

Instead, each time I return from the reddening meadow, I patter to the pantry now and peek at the preserves, pry open the freezer for some quick reassurance that the berries are still here. Huddled together on the shelf, the summertime relics remind. I look at them stacked up in the freezer and see my feet walking toward their meadow, over and past the lichen-covered rocks, dew on the grass, the morning sun already hot on my back.

"Will it be pie, then, or a pudding?" I ask myself.

With such a bountiful stash, I consider an old fashioned coffee cake called a buckle, so named due to the copious amounts of berries in the batter—so many, in fact, that the cake "buckles" in the middle. I try to imagine a season without the berries and cringe at the thought. While I'm a fool for a single berry plucked and popped into the mouth, its sun-warmed juices squirting over tongue, the rich tradition of simply prepared fruit desserts equally tempts and teases. Shortcakes and custards, crisps and crumbles, flummeries and fools, they're what get us through those times when what we really need is something sweet.

The berries are still on my mind as I rummage around in the cabinet and retrieve the heavy-bottomed pan I used all summer for making jam. To make a blueberry "slump," the fruit is combined with a bit of water and sugar in a heavy pan and brought to a boil. A quick, sweet dumpling batter is then dropped by the spoonful over the simmering berries. Cover tightly and steam until the dumplings are cooked through. Serve warm in bowls with a little cream drizzled over.

While the little indigo gems do remind of summer, they have become so much more than that to me: an assurance of sweetness itself. They have become a kind of window to the past, a gateway to memory, a harbinger of our ever-ripening days. There were even moments in the meadow when something, perhaps the sweet berries themselves, insistently whispered to me: heaven exists. I found myself, kneeling beneath berry branch, wondering whether I truly believed that statement, could ever believe it to be true, and if so, what it's implications in my life might be.

What would it mean to say that, yes, I believe? Or to consider and embrace just as fervently the alternative?

My father once caught a glimpse of heaven when he was still a small boy. He had been playing with his twin brother in the sloping backyard of his childhood home. Next door the neighbors had decided the day was perfect to burn off that brush pile they had stacked in the corner of their lot. When the neighbor boys invited the twins over to the crackling pile of branches, Ray gleefully scampered over the fence. What happened next isn't entirely clear, but either he was pushed or he fell into the flames.

Whenever my father attempted to tell the next part of this story, he would more often than not simply give up. It was crystal clear in his head, but putting that highly saturated memory into words was another thing altogether. He might whisper something about a sweet peacefulness enveloping him, or something about being somewhere painfully beautiful. But no words could ever describe what he had experienced, he would inevitably say. Then he would drift off, lost in the crucible of memory.

How long my father was gone that terrible fiery day—whether several seconds, an excruciating minute, or even longer—I cannot say, but the moment remained kindled in his memory well after he finally awoke to his mother changing the dressings on his badly burned little body. He carried it always, as well as the scars of that flame-induced vision, to the very end of his life.

There are various growing seasons about the green earth. But those moments can be frozen in time, or at least mercifully slowed down. Wonderfully sweet combinations can be created in the jam pot when batches of fruit are frozen fresh at their peak. A few icy blueberries tossed into the autumn-ripe pears make for an intriguing preserve. A favorite combination is made possible only by fooling time and making use of the freezer, bringing together the tart, tender stalks of early spring rhubarb and those luscious late-summer berries of blue. The jams will find their way into any number of dishes: warmed gently to slide down a scoop of ice cream, slathered over sweet crepes drizzled with maple syrup, swirled into yogurt, glazed atop a fresh fruit pie, or tucked into the middle of a heavenly crumb cake.

The seeker and the scientist have this in common: so much of what they desire to know remains beyond their grasp. Both operate in the possibility of possibility. We have inherited inquiring, analytical brains that are also capable, frustratingly so, of embracing transcendent belief. The problem is that truth is never absolute and more plural than any of us are comfortable with. That and the fact that belief is something we can never measure or prove. And in the realm of belief, well, proof isn't even the point.

But then we head out into the world where every other person, directed by his or her own analytical and awe-seeking brain, has beliefs of his or her own that may or may not agree with ours. The work is to hold onto certain truths without condemning anyone who does not hold the same beliefs to be true; to hold onto our beliefs without being held captive by them. I am reminded of how poorly we practice this every time I read or listen to the daily news. I may pray for peace and reconciliation every day, yet what I find over and over again is not a decrease in unrest and inhumanity, but a terrible increase of improvised explosive devices, pre-emptive strikes and mutual deterrents. And yet I still want to believe with all my heart the words I whisper into the air at the start and end of each day: on earth as it is in heaven.

To make a blueberry fool, simply beat whipping cream until soft peaks form. Gently fold in jam made from wild blueberries ripened in the summer sun. Add a splash of cassis if desired, or a few gratings of cinnamon or nutmeg. Spoon into parfait glasses and serve chilled.

Is it possible to find revelation, to find faith, in a tiny blue berry? My wild meadow reveries so often leave me not steadfast and sure, but wondering and questioning. What is the very nature of truth itself? Or of memory? What *do* I believe, and why? Is there any room for doubt in a life of faith? If heaven is, will we ever find it, and where and when will that be? We may not want to think about it, but there is an inherent element of uncertainty within faith, a great deal more doubt than desired. I wonder, though, whether we've defined the words inadequately, contrasted faith and doubt in such a way that we automatically make of them antonyms when they're more likely something synonymous or more. There seems to be an implied comfort in faith, that the certainty of faith can and will remove any and all doubt. But faith is a risky business; there's the possibility of both hope and failure in every act of faith.

Nearly eight decades after his first glimpse of heaven, my father finally went there. I cannot prove this. Yet as I sat with him the night before he died, I could sense his conviction, feel how hard he was working to get there. He knew where he was going and went there determinedly. It wasn't easy. In my memory I often return to that night and the moment after I had said good-bye to him and turned to look at him from the doorway one last time. The memory allows me what the moment did not: the possibility of letting myself linger there even longer in the doorway of his room. And what I see now is that there is also a good deal of courage in faith.

I may never have proof that my father arrived at that achingly beautiful place that haunted his memory, or know whether or not his vision of heaven was accurate. I can only hope that he was right to believe in it, and trust that whoever whispered into my ear in the blueberry meadow was correct: that heaven exists, that what is gone is not gone forever, and that faith, like memory, endures.

www.ingramcontent.com/pod-product-compliance
Lightning Source LLC
Chambersburg PA
CBHW071106090426
42737CB00013B/2501